EMBRACING CHANGE

Embracing Change, Spirituality and the Lindisfarne Gospels.

© Ewan Clayton and Robert Cooper.

First published in 2003 by Ewan Clayton,

15 Sillwood Road, Brighton, BN1 2LF.

ISBN 0-9545507-0-6

Designed by Ewan Clayton.

Printed by Evonprint, Small Dole, West Sussex.

With thanks to The British Library

for their permission to reproduce

the images from the Lindisfarne Gospels,

BL Cotton Ms Nero D.iv.

Thanks also to Fenwick Lawson

for allowing Robert Cooper's image of

Cuthbert of Farne to be reproduced.

This book is set in the Adobe Minion

type family with Jovica Veljovic's

Silentium Pro being used for the title page,

a letterform developed from later Anglo-Saxon

manuscripts of the tenth century.

The river is within us, the sea is all about us;

The sea is the land's edge also, the granite

Into which it reaches, the beaches where it tosses

Its hints of earlier and other creation…

Dry Salvages, The Four Quartets. T.S.Eliot

EMBRACING CHANGE

Spirituality and the Lindisfarne Gospels

Written by Ewan Clayton, with photography of Holy Island by Robert Cooper

Foreword

The Lindisfarne Gospel Book was written in St.Cuthbert's memory by one of his monks, Eadfrith. For many years it was displayed close to Cuthbert's tomb in the church on Lindisfarne. Today it can be seen in the British Library in London. It remains an eloquent witness to the good news about a God who is 'with us', everywhere and through all time. Since 1988 Robert Cooper and I have led calligraphy retreats on the island of Lindisfarne, or Holy Island as it is named locally. Robert is a chaplain to the Arts in the North East of England and a photographer, I am a calligrapher. Our intention in making this book is simply to share some of the insights that have come to us during these annual times for reflection. This is not a scholarly work but rather a collection of meditations and stories based loosely around an extraordinary manuscript and the bleak, bare island that was its home. In some ways the reflective process we hope to stimulate is similar to the kind of work that the Lindisfarne Gospel Book was originally designed to encourage. Robert's photographs are all taken on Lindisfarne. They set the manuscript in the context for which it was written: a journey of faith on a remarkable island that teaches its own, challenging, lessons.

Whilst this is not an academic work, it is indebted to the ideas of others. I would mention in particular Michelle Brown of the British Library and Canon Kate Tristram, who lives on Holy Island. What I have written about hermits in early Anglo-Saxon England in particular is drawn from the talks Kate has given at our calligraphy retreats. Robert and I would say that our ideas and our pictures are only as they are because of the world she has opened up for us through her knowledge and her consummate gift for story telling. So it is to Kate that, with affection and respect, we would like to dedicate this book. A final word of thanks to the islanders themselves. Over the years we have visited we have always been met with kindness and smiles. Many of the families on the island have lived there for centuries. It is their place, their home. Thank you for sharing it.

Ewan Clayton, March 20th 2003

6

Introduction

The Lindisfarne Gospel Book is one of the great manuscripts of the early Middle Ages. Like all significant books it is a reflection of the community that made it. By looking at it carefully, we can discover something of the community that conceived and created it and gain insight into their aspirations and beliefs. This is the purpose of this small, meditative book, to take a great work of calligraphy and show how it arises from an entire way of life and a stance towards one's own humanity. The manuscript is a marvel of accomplished craftsmanship, but far more striking is the wellspring of the human spirit from which its rivers and whirlpools, its meres and oceans of decoration and writing flowed, day after day, form after form. It is from this living stream of water that I encourage you to drink.

The exact dates of the manuscript's commission and completion are not known. Until recently many scholars accepted that the work took at least two years to complete and that it was finished in 698 – to coincide with the translation of St. Cuthbert's remains. This 'translation' was the moment when his body was taken from the ground to be reburied in the same church in a more splendid shrine, thus celebrating his sanctity. Recent discussions about why and when the book was written suggest a later date. Michelle Brown in her *2000 Jarrow Lecture*, argued that the book was probably written over a more extended period and may even have been left unfinished on the death of its scribe Eadfrith in 721.

The context in which Michelle places the creation of the book is not that of Cuthbert's translation. Instead she relates it to a concern shared by the Lindisfarne community and Bede's monastery of Wearmouth and Jarrow to portray Cuthbert as unifier of Irish (Columban), English, Roman and indeed universal Christian traditions. Seen in this light, Bede's

Life of Cuthbert (one in verse and one in prose) and his *History of the English Church and People* stand alongside the Lindisfarne Gospels as part of this programme. So, when I comment on the links between Cuthbert's life as represented by Bede and the details of the composition of the Gospel Book itself, I am aware I may be reading back into Cuthbert's life the concern of these two contemporary communities to stress Cuthbert as 'the great Reconciler'. But this picture may not be too far from the truth. Bede built his portrait from eye-witness accounts. He was writing during a period when many who remembered Cuthbert were still alive. His lives of Cuthbert represent an accumulation of individual reflections on what Cuthbert's presence in their midst had meant to those who knew him, and the implications of this for following a Christian way of life in their time. By looking at Cuthbert's life, the island that was his home and the Gospel Book written to honour his memory, I hope you too will be stimulated to reflect on what this tradition means to you, not in an art historical sense, but in terms of your own spirituality and thirst for life.

So what is the heart of this book? My concern is for what the Lindisfarne Gospel Book can say now about the human journey. It seems to me that, as in any human relationship, artistic achievement also requires a partly prior and partly simultaneous enlargement of the individual's capacity to embrace 'the Other'. This is a psycho-physical achievement which engages us at the most profound level. So the interesting question for an artist to ask is what enables this process of engagement and enlargement to happen? And the artistically creative question to ask of any historical artefact is not simply how it was made or even why it was made, but how did it come to be humanly possible to make it?

So now we are ready to begin our journey, tracing the footprints of Cuthbert and his community across the shifting sands towards Holy Island. Perhaps your heart, like mine, is full of expectation – we will not be disappointed....

A Journey begins

To walk into the world reflected in the Gospel Book, I invite you now to join me in a journey of the imagination. We begin on the shores of the place known as Holy Island where, some thirteen hundred years ago, our manuscript was made. The island lies just off the east coast of northern England, close to the border with Scotland. At high tide it is cut off from the mainland by a strip of water a mile or more wide, but at low tide it rejoins the mainland once more and is accessible across a wide stretch of sands. For centuries travellers have followed this route to the island's small settlement.

It was here in the year 635 AD that Irish monks from Iona, led by a man called Aidan, began a Christian mission to Northumbria at the invitation of its King. Some thirty years later it also became home to a monk called Cuthbert, whose warm personality, gifts of healing and inspired leadership brought him a fame which continues to this day. For centuries people have been drawn to the places where he and his community lived – some in search of healing, some for advice, some no doubt prompted by a deep, but unidentified, longing. As you look at the image opposite, I invite you to imagine yourself as one of them.

The posts in the picture mark the Pilgrim's Way across the sands to Holy Island. Give yourself time to let this image sink in. Can you smell the salt in the air? Listen to the sound of the water slowly receding, the sands sighing and popping, breathing. Let us imagine that you have journeyed on purpose to this place. You stand here, on the edge of something new. You stand where a track-way meets the sand in seaweed, grass and rock. Many of your brothers and sisters have also stood here – on the edge – when they came to this same place centuries ago. You pause on the shoreline.

Do all journeys begin with a question?

Out here on the sandy flats, deserts of water and sky,

everything seems open to question

But just as you feel ready to start towards your destination, the fog sweeps in. Suddenly, it is cold and lonely. Perhaps you are anxious, aware of a weight you are carrying, burdens of ill-health, responsibilities or difficult decisions. As the fog thickens you begin to lose your grip on why you came in the first place. Questions arise. Will I find a welcome? Will the journey, the effort, be worth it? Wouldn't it be simpler just to turn back? But something draws you on. Extraordinary though it seems, you step forward into this fog! Deep down it seems you *are* looking for something. Is it peace? Answers? Strength? Gentleness? The re-awakening of feelings after a time of being numbed? Or is it change, healing, new life, new energy, new hope, new love?

What are *you* looking for?

There is an edge of danger here also, and mystery, but the posts left by the people who travelled this way before offer themselves as guides. The landscape is bleak, exposed. But surely if love, contentment and joy can be found, even in this uncomfortable place, then they can be found anywhere.

13

As you walk on, the clouds lift. Eventually you reach a beach of stones and, leaving the main path into the village, you decide to turn right; picking your way along the base of a shallow cliff, a gentle bay opens before you. Here you turn inland up a stony path. There is a church, houses, and somewhere, close by a tiny harbour, you hope you may find rest and a welcome. Perhaps at last you will discover something of the truth you have travelled this far to see.

Who are you looking for?

There is a timelessness to the scene in front of you now and you begin to imagine you are walking this same pathway centuries ago. As you finish the short climb, a bell begins to sound. You are aware of movement amongst the buildings. People are emerging and a procession is forming, which makes its way towards the sound of the bell. The final figure in the procession turns towards you, smiles and beckons. You follow into the dimness of a wooden church. As the monks chant, another procession moves forward, led by a cross. After the cross walk monks with candles and then, last of all, borne gently but joyfully, comes an open book, its colours glowing in the candlelight. Silence falls as a monk begins to read in Latin, he is almost singing, he knows the words by heart:

In principio erat verbum, et verbum erat apud Deum.
In the beginning was the Word, and the Word was with God and the Word was God

After the book has been placed reverently on the altar, an old monk speaks, again in Latin. As he does so, there is a nodding of heads, smiles and even occasional laughter. Two names keep cropping up in his speech, 'Christus' and 'Cuthbertus'. It is difficult to make much of his words, but one thing seems clear, whatever it was that these monks came here seeking, appears to have been met by a combination of this book, its holy 'Word' and this man Cuthbert. What is the secret of this community's obvious optimism? Why do these men seem so intensely alive? How can it be that they already appear to have opened a space and a genuine welcome for us?

We know that very many people made just such a journey during St. Cuthbert's lifetime, seeking his help or advice, both of which he gave generously. 'He welcomed every inquiring heart' says his contemporary, the Venerable Bede, in his *History of the English Church and People*. Thanks to Bede, who also wrote both a verse and a prose life of St. Cuthbert, we know a good deal about this down-to-earth, holy and humorous man. The more I have read the stories about him and the more I have looked at the Lindisfarne Gospels, the clearer it seems to me that there is a link between the two. But these connections go deeper than Aldred's inscription, added after he had inserted the Anglo-Saxon translation between the Latin lines of the text, that the manuscript had been made 'for God and St. Cuthbert'. Later on in this book I will outline the nature of these connections but we will understand them better if we first try to look beneath the events of Cuthbert's life, at Cuthbert the human being.

Cuthbert, the down-to-earth saint

As Cuthbert's story unfolds, what emerges from Bede's pen is a picture of a man, probably of relatively high birth, who enjoyed popularity even as a child. He was strong and fit, with a naturally engaging personality. After a night-time vision during which he believed that he had seen angels welcoming a human soul 'marvellously bright' into heaven, he committed himself to life as a monk. From then on, his natural gifts of communication were directed into the work of sharing the Christian gospel. According to Bede, 'the love of heavenly joys' moved him to become an outstanding and enthusiastic preacher who did not restrict his teaching and influence to the monastery, but 'worked to rouse up the ordinary folk far and near'. He was also a courageous and accepting person, who 'used to visit and preach mainly in the villages that lay far distant among high and inaccessible mountains, which others feared to visit'.

For love of heavenly joys...

Cuthbert's Island, his first hermitage

The faith that
works by love . . .

18

However, it is above all the warmth of Cuthbert's personality that comes down to us in the stories about him, stories that are still told in the northern part of England that was his home. Significantly, Cuthbert's first responsibility in monastic life was as the guest master. This was a job where warmth, practical generosity and the ability to welcome all-comers (however awkward!) were essential. Perhaps these were to some extent Cuthbert's natural qualities, but perhaps they were also learned, as one account of a crucial moment in his formation as a monk suggests. This was the time when he seems to have fallen under the spell of the Gospel of St. John. Bede records that as Boisil (Cuthbert's friend and master) lay dying of plague, he and Cuthbert read through the whole of a commentary on St. John together. They used a little book with seven gatherings of pages and read one gathering each day during the last week of Boisil's life. They were able to read and discuss this with relative ease and speed says Bede, 'because they dealt only with the simple things of "the faith that works by love" (Gal: 5,3) and not deep matters of dispute'. The challenge to centre his life on 'the faith that works by love', seems to have left a deep impression on Cuthbert. It was his last lesson from his father in the monastic life that his way of life as a monk and a Christian was not to be based on sets of rules or abstract propositions, but on active participation in life, in practical charity and loving response. That this was a lived reality for Cuthbert can be seen at several points in Bede's description of him. For instance 'He regarded it as equivalent to prayer to help the weaker brethren with advice, remembering that He who said, "Thou shalt love the Lord thy God" also said, "Love thy neighbour"'. We see it also in Bede's frequent references to the way in which Cuthbert taught not just by word, but also by example, in fact he says this every single time he mentions Cuthbert teaching.

Preserve among yourselves unfailing charity,

reach unanimity in your decisions – receive those who come to you with kindness, despise no-one…

from Bede's record of Cuthbert's last wishes for his community.

Another of Cuthbert's qualities seems to have been a gift for empathy. When people were with Cuthbert they discovered someone who really had time for them. He listened. In Bede's words, 'he was unassumingly patient and kindly to all who came to him for comfort'. Most significantly, people seem to have felt that they were in the presence of someone with whom they could be totally honest: 'none presumed to hide their inmost secrets from him, but all openly confessed their wrong doing; for they felt it impossible to conceal their guilt from him'. Have you ever had this experience? You meet someone who is so down to earth and honest about themselves that you find you no longer need to pretend, you are free to be yourself and discover the amazing experience of being accepted as you are. This can change everything. The past is open to healing, and you come to experience a new wholeness and self-respect, which is at the same time a liberating awareness of an interdependence of being with others.

This ability – to experience and communicate, in Christian terms, the mysterious and liberating power of love and forgiveness – is seen in many incidents in Cuthbert's life. It was one of his foremost qualities. Bede reveals he was frequently given to tears when listening to the stories of other people's lives, 'often as they were pouring out their sins he would be the first to burst into tears, tears of sympathy' and then he would offer to do their penance himself!

Where did Cuthbert's understanding of forgiveness and his gift for empathy come from? To a certain extent these qualities must have been natural to him, they were obviously valued parts of his experience of his own humanity, but I believe that they were certainly reinforced by the hermit's vocation towards which he was drawn and for which other members of the Lindisfarne community continually offered themselves. Why should this have been so?

A mysterious and liberating power

The American monk, Thomas Merton, has described the contemplative life as 'an advance into solitude, a confrontation with poverty and the void, a renunciation of your idea of yourself in the presence of death and nothingness, in order to overcome all the confusion of ignorance and error that spring from the fear of being nothing.' (Rain and the Rhinoceros, in *Raids on the Unspeakable*, p.15, London: Burns and Oates, 1977.)

Merton, who lived as a hermit for the last few years of his life, goes on to say that 'emptiness and apparent uselessness' are in fact the necessary conditions for an encounter with Truth. In this desert, when all the unattractive sides of yourself come bubbling up in ever different and fantasized shapes (as ways of avoiding this encounter) you survive only by learning to love yourself and this means learning to forgive. And, of course, if you can forgive yourself, it comes naturally to you to forgive others. Such, I believe was the generous truth that Cuthbert encountered in the solitariness of his life as a hermit.

Cuthbert moved to the Farne Islands, a few miles further out to sea from Holy Island, to be a full-time hermit after ten years spent on Lindisfarne as Prior; a time which itself had followed ten years based in the monastery at Melrose. He had in fact already spent some extended periods in solitude on the little island, still known as St. Cuthbert's Island, that lies in the sandy bay next to the monastery on Lindisfarne. But for the last period of his life solitude became a full-time commitment. People still sought him out and he, ever attentive to their needs, built them a small guest house near his simple landing stage on the Inner Farne.

Today, the hermit's vocation might strike us as a self-indulgent withdrawal from the world, but this would be very far from the understanding of Cuthbert's own day. Then, hermits were understood to have been called to go further into the

22

Emptiness
and apparent
uselessness
are necessary
conditions
for an
encounter
with truth

heart of the battle between good and evil, by allowing their own inner life and faithfulness to God to become the front-line of this conflict. Cuthbert's choice of the island of Inner Farne for his hermitage therefore had little to do with a desire to escape or retreat in search of peace. On the contrary, according to the understanding of the time, Bede tells us that he chose it because it had the reputation for being the island in the area most thickly infested with demons. Here then was not a place of peace but a focus of the conflict with evil. Spiritually this represented an enormous risk. Christians such as Cuthbert were convinced that the ultimate victory had been won through Christ's death on the cross; they had no doubt that good would triumph. But they also recognized that in this struggle individuals could still get seriously hurt and even lost. However, when any Christian successfully persisted in this interior struggle, the victory was believed to belong not to them, but to the whole Church. This was why the hermit's vocation undertaken by Cuthbert was valued so much.

The reality of Cuthbert's ability both to love and to forgive had already been tested when he was first sent to Lindisfarne as Prior of the monastery. The circumstances of his appointment meant that he was walking into conflict. He had come to Lindisfarne following the Synod of Whitby in 664, which had settled the dispute between the Irish-Columban and the Roman church concerning various traditions: for example the way in which the date of Easter should be set. At Whitby, Colman, Bishop and Abbot of Lindisfarne, had argued the case for the Irish ways and lost. The Roman case, argued by Wilfrid, won. Many of the Lindisfarne monks found this cultural change unacceptable and Colman led the majority of the community back to Ireland. Unsurprisingly, when Cuthbert was sent from Melrose to Lindisfarne to care for those who had remained, he found a community rent by internal division. Each day Cuthbert went to the community meeting where, with good humour, he patiently presented his suggested way forward. To begin with no one listened and when the meetings degenerated into argument, he would smile and leave, unruffled, returning the next day to continue his course of gentle persuasion. Eventually his patience and steady optimism won through.

*Walking
into conflict*

*learning
to forgive…*

oneself.

Cuthbert's ability to bring about reconciliation should perhaps be seen as part of the healing gift for which he was most famed. Miraculous powers are often attributed to such charismatic figures and Cuthbert was no exception. Whilst some may wish to question the exact nature of the events, or treat them symbolically, they still reveal much about Cuthbert's character and spirituality.

Sheer gift

spring after spring after spring

this happens

A recurring theme that I see in the miracle stories that gathered around Cuthbert is his appreciation of the unreckonable giftedness of creation. For example, Cuthbert frequently finds he is provided for: a bird drops a fish out of the sky when he is hungry; a loaf of bread is left in a surprising place and discovered by his horse; three slices of dolphin flesh appear when he is stranded on a beach in a snowstorm. Even this next story of the uneaten goose, dating from Cuthbert's last days, speaks to me of this outlook on life.

In this later story, told to Bede by Cynimund (one of the monks who had been there) Cuthbert has been unwell and some members of the community on Lindisfarne sails over to visit him in his hermitage. Cuthbert generously gives them a goose and invites them to eat it. Later they decide this is unnecessary – they have enough food. A great wind rises and for the next few days they are trapped on the island unable to sail home. I guess every day they look at the goose, but they stick to their principles and it remains uneaten. Later, when Cuthbert calls in to see how they are, he notices the goose is still there. Like a true Desert Father he offers them a word to live by – they really should have listened to him, God had in fact provided a pleasant meal for them but apparently they knew better and had turned Him down! No wonder they had then got stuck on the island facing the uneaten meal for several days!

Bede's account preserves a curious short comment from his original witness that gives us an additional insight into Cuthbert's reaction. He says Cuthbert calmly upbraided them, and then adds, 'he was, in fact, rather pleased'. I imagine Cuthbert grinning, and recognise this from my own time in a monastery as typical of a particular kind of monk's self-deprecating humour, full of warmth and experience. Using humour as loving correction or teaching is normal monastic behaviour. Cuthbert is grinning because this is the lesson we never seem to learn – he is saying 'you are making things so much harder for yourself than they need to be! Get out of your head, and move into the reality of the situation - this is where God is. The right thing to do is usually very simple and straightforward and always under our noses. Think of your situation – seven days facing an uneaten goose! And all so completely unnecessary, you could have had a lovely dinner!'

Bede conveys the tale to us as a simple lesson in obedience. Indeed it is a beautifully nuanced reaction and it shines with Cuthbert's teaching that life is full of gifts and that God speaks to us through this. Acceptance of the miracle of everyday life is a basic spiritual lesson. Choosing not to live this graced existence can lead to congestion of the spirit – no sense of gift, no real engagement with life, no dynamic relationship with God. 'No wonder you lot got stuck!' Here then was a man of prayer who was no stranger to the human heart, who recognised anxiety, sickness, dread, shame, evasion - a man with whom people could be themselves – really deeply themselves – and find that it was all right! The effect in many cases was transformative. People who visited him left for home with the sense that they had really met with some kind of healing and forgiveness. Bede says, 'no-one left unconsoled; no-one had to carry back the burdens he came with.' The quality of Cuthbert's presence appears to have enabled people to let go of their burdens and engage with what the contemporary theologian Walter Breugermann has called 'the promise of newness' in their lives. After spending time with Cuthbert people felt able to begin again, capable of loving and being loved.

...the God of surprises!

30

Of course, such stories as these about Cuthbert probably get exaggerated in the telling. Doubtless, Cuthbert had his faults his very real humanity makes that all the more certain! There are good reasons, however, for believing that Cuthbert was genuinely a rather remarkable person, not just because of his personal qualities, but also because of the way these qualities influenced the lives of others and gave shape to the community he later came to lead. Human encounters undergirded the community that produced this gospel book. The Christian Church in Northumbria was generated by such encounters as was the community on Lindisfarne itself. It is through the lens of human relationships and a shared search for God that we need to view the material pages of the book which came to be dedicated to Cuthbert's memory.

The man and the book – making connections

Having learnt something about the life of this unusual man what happens if we take what we know and look at the pages of the Lindisfarne Gospels through this lens? Are there any ways in which Cuthbert's life, or that of the community he inspired, can be seen to be reflected in its conception? In what ways might we be able to continue to use the book today?

We have already noted many deeply human qualities emerging from Bede's pen-portrait of St. Cuthbert. Is it a coincidence that the Lindisfarne Gospel Book is the first manuscript from the British Isles to show the gospel writers Matthew, Mark, Luke and John as real human beings? Earlier books had only ever represented them by their symbols. More intriguingly St. John appears to receive special treatment. We know that Cuthbert's spirituality seems to have been rooted in a special relationship with St. John's gospel, as evidenced in that formative week with the dying Boisil. Moreover, a copy of this gospel was found with Cuthbert's body when his coffin was opened in the early middle ages. It can be seen today on loan

How well do you know the truth of your own heart?

to the British Library. In the Lindisfarne Gospels St. John has his name lettered twice as high as the other evangelists and with a decorated infilling, and of all the evangelists, John alone is shown, not writing or in sideways view, but with his hand over his heart and facing the reader directly. He looks at us straight out of the page as if to say, 'I teach from the heart and from the reality of my presence'. At this period in history this way of representing John was unique in Insular (Irish and British) art, though it does appear also carved on Cuthbert's wooden coffin preserved today in the Cathedral Treasury at Durham. In thus portraying John, who was Cuthbert's inspiration, the scribe reminds us of the inspiration of Cuthbert, who likewise practised 'the faith which works by love' - teaching from the heart and an authoratitive presence.

On the very last page of the Lindisfarne manuscript today there is an inscription written by Aldred, a priest in the community at Chester-le-Street. The community from Lindisfarne had settled there for a while in the ninth century after their flight from the island as a result of continuing Viking attacks. Aldred was responsible for the little interlinear writing which translates the Latin text of the Gospel book into Anglo-Saxon. In the inscription at the back of the manuscript he records that Eadfrith wrote the book, Ethelwald bound it and Billfrith decorated the binding with metal work and jewels. What appears significant to me from this fact is the human element to the inscription: well over a century after the book was written this community still clearly had a memory for individuals.

I teach from the heart, from the reality of my presence

Significant passages

Throughout the Lindisfarne Gospels there are passages of the text that are highlighted in various ways, usually with simple washes of colour or lines of dots around the opening letters of these passages; this artistic treatment has been called the secondary decoration of the manuscript. There are several passages like this in the Gospel Book; their special decorative treatment can be explained in all but a few cases by the prominent place of the text in the Church's calendar. For some passages there is no obvious liturgical explanation as to why they called forth this slightly more elaborate treatment. When taken together however and recalled in the context of what we have already learned of Cuthbert's life these passages could be read as an evocation of Cuthbert's particular gifts and insights. Perhaps by marking these passages out, Cuthbert's spiritual sons are being encouraged to continue to imitate his example. Certainly we, as latter day readers, might care to read these verses and reflect on them for ourselves in this context.

The texts in question are: the Beatitudes, Matthew 5, 3-11, the Parable of the Prodigal Son, Luke 15, 11, the Temptation of Jesus in the wilderness, Luke 4, 1, the story of the Widow of Nain, Luke 7,11, and Luke 5,1 and 27, the story of the calling of the disciples to follow Christ. The Beatitudes all begin, 'How blessed' or 'How happy'. They are the preaching of the good news par excellence. What better passage than Christ's great sermon could we chose to recall this optimistic preacher and pastor who spoke 'for love of heavenly joys'? The Parable of the Prodigal Son is Christ's great account of lavish forgiveness. Based on what we have learnt about Cuthbert, this is clearly a passage that takes us directly to the heart of his own spiritual practice. The Temptation of Jesus in the wilderness is, of course, the archetypal description of the hermit's vocation, to which Cuthbert himself was drawn. Its final passage 'Angels came and ministered to him' also recalls the many stories of angelic intervention that surrounded him. And in the story of the widow of Nain, the widow's son is raised from the dead and 'given back to his mother', just as Cuthbert's body after eleven years in the grave was discovered by the community to be miraculously incorrupt, a sign of the resurrection life and of how 'God had visited them' also. This was the life, an imitation of Christ, that Cuthbert's spiritual sons were invited to follow.

Sun on the road after rain,
a path that leads both towards the castle
and away from it.

Spirituality and change

For me, such chance connections illustrate one of the ways we might use the book in our own spiritual practice today. The Lindisfarne Gospels can still be food for meditative reading in the Benedictine tradition of *lectio divina*, the slow rumination on passages of scripture in relation to each other and to the events of our daily lives (read in translation but pointed to by contemplating the original manuscript). The book could be read as a map, operating on many levels, charting the spiritual landfalls by which we ourselves, as latter day sons and daughters of Cuthbert, are encouraged to navigate our paths towards (or within) God; a path Cuthbert himself followed in his own imitation of Christ and the saints. This perspective is quite separate from the scholarly one that places the book in the context of a cult object, subject to complex political and social considerations and programmes, but it can sit alongside it. Books in our libraries and museums can still be read this way today. However, I believe that Cuthbert's primary influence on this book lies at an even deeper generative level. Humanly speaking his particular genius for sanctity, and his spiritual direction of the community, seems to have been crucial in that enlargement of the spirit that I spoke of in the introduction and without which no substantially new artistic achievement seems possible. This question leads naturally to the issue of Cuthbert's spirituality.

What is spirituality? Spirituality is not a thing, it is a process, a dimension of human existence, a search, an ongoing life-long journey – it is concerned with the way we face the big questions in life, how we deal with death, illness, despair, uncontainable joy, the ups and downs of our relationships with others, beginnings and endings. If you related at all to the meditation on the Pilgrims' Way and the path across to Lindisfarne in the fog, you already know what spirituality means. It is the ability to ask existential questions and to shape your life in response to the insights that arise in the sometimes alarming space they open up.

Spirituality is therefore most definitely not a system of beliefs – that is theology or philosophy. Spirituality is to do with our everyday practice, in other words with how we actually behave in relation to the great questions; how we behave when faced by disappointment, by illness, by death. In each of these situations, coming to us in all their concrete detail, in our unique life, how do we find ways of engaging with the 'God who is with us' and so discover in everything the promise of newness and meaning? Significantly, there is a common thread which runs through all these challenges – and that is the way in which we deal with ongoing *change*.

It is as we reflect on change that the Lindisfarne Gospel Book gives us a remarkable insight into the community of St. Cuthbert. Here we can glimpse something of the book's real glory, something that is ultimately even more sustaining than the exquisite craftsmanship and miraculous writing. That we can glimpse this 'something' is because any book is inevitably connected to the achievements of the human heart. What we are witness to in this book is the struggle of Cuthbert and his community to walk in the freedom and love which was its calling – a calling which at this particular time in history could only be embraced through change.

It possible for us to experience this dimension of the community's life because, as many art historians and paleographers will tell you, one of the most striking aspects of the book is precisely this – how it handles change. Several earlier manuscripts written on Lindisfarne, or centres associated with it, allow us to make comparisons which reveal how the Lindisfarne Gospel Book marks a new moment in the history of book production in the 'Insular' tradition. Let us look at several innovations in turn.

How do you embrace change?

In the beginning was the Word

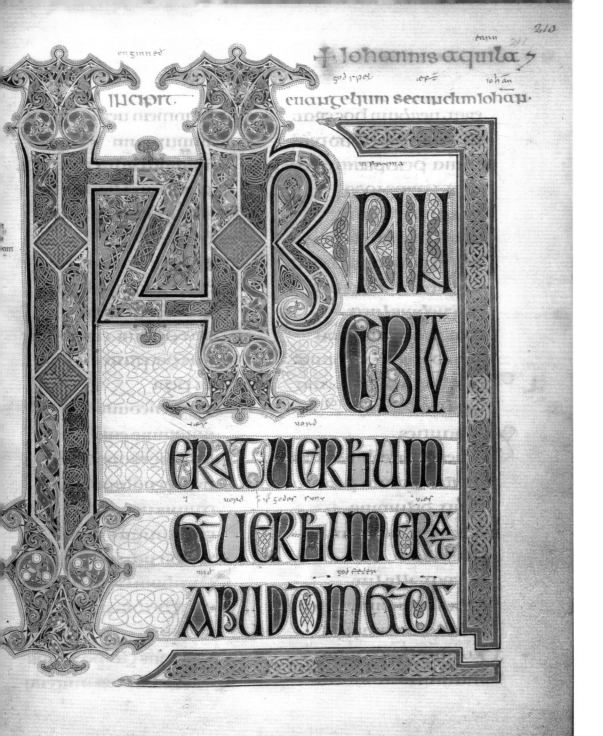

...and the Word was with God

To begin with, as I have already mentioned, in a striking departure from tradition, each gospel opens with a portrait of the evangelist. Previously the gospel writers had been portrayed only by their symbols - a lion for Mark, an angel for Matthew, a calf for Luke and an eagle for John. Here, for the first time they appear as human beings. Never before had they been depicted in this way in any manuscript from the British Isles.

The carpet pages (pages of elaborate decoration that open each gospel) reveal another development. Their equivalent in the Book of Durrow (made at the very least forty years earlier) appear purely decorative. Now we are presented with a series of Cross pages. And as I look at how this book is organized – a repeated three-fold pattern of first, a portrait of the evangelist, then a cross-carpet page and finally the gospel text – I am aware that I am looking at the visual equivalent of the way in which the missionaries from Holy Island are known to have begun their preaching in the surrounding countryside. On entering a village these evangelists would have set up a cross, presented themselves as witnesses to its message and then, 'for love of heavenly joys', proclaimed the gospel.

In parallel to all this engagement with change went a programme of technical inniovation in the making of the manuscript. The script used to write the book is the first surviving example of a new and much more regular form of half-uncial writing: a style the scholar Julian Brown identified as Phase II. The letters are more unified and uniform, the penmanship is crisper, the serifs – the beginnings and endings of the strokes – are sharp and quite pronounced. Clarity pervades the page. This is the result, perhaps, of seeing new manuscripts in uncials imported from Italy, or made at the nearby

…and he will give you another counsellor

to be with you forever…the spirit of truth

who is with you and who is in you.

reda gelefor manse
QUI CREDIT INME
yoepco da ic vyco
OPERA QUAE EGO FACIO
y he pyncad
ET IPSE FACIET
y damna dana t dyna
ET MAIORA HORUM
pyncap fte ic
FACIET QUIA EGO
to diem foden ic gie t.
AD PATREM UADO
y rya hued giegebiddep
ET QUOD CUM q; PETI
onoma minu
ERITIS INNOMINE MEO
dip ic vyco .t. ic doat.
HOC FACIAM
fte gewloned re defeden
UT GLORIFICETUR PATER
infilio
INFILIO
gir hued giegegnad .t. mec
SI QUID PETIERITIS ME
onoma minu
INNOMINE MEO
dip ic doat .t. ic vyco
HOC FACIAM
gie gie gelyfap mec
SI DILIGUS ME
bebod mino
MANDATA MEA
behaldap gie
SERUATE
y ic gebidd done-foden
ET EGO ROGABO PATREM
y odenne numod t.
ET ALIUM PARACLETUM
gepilid mid ivh
DABIT UOBIS
fte gewna mid ivh
UT MANEAT UOBIS CUM
in mec nyye
INAETERNUM
sart rod...niyer done
SPM UERITATIS QUEM
middan nemage
MUNDUS NON POTEST

onfoa
ACCIPERE
fdon negerud hine
QUIA NON UIDET EUM
ne yat hine
NEC SCIT EUM
gie vyt ongeattap
UOS AUTEM COGNOSCITIS
hine fdon mid ivh
EUM QUIA APUD UOS
vynap y inivh bid
MANEBIT ET INUOBIS ERIT
ne fleto ivh
NON RELINQUAM UOS
fnonoleapa .t. aldonleapa t.
ORFANOS
ic cymmo to ivh
UENIAM ADUOS
gtc lytel t.
ADHUC MODICUM
y remido mec
ET MUNDUS ME
gtc t. negerud
IAM NON UIDET
gie vyt gie geteap mec
UOS AUTEM UIDEATIS ME
fte t. fdon ic lifo
QUIA EGO UIUO
y gie lifiap
ET UOS UIUETIS
ondem deege gie ongeattap
INILLO DIE UOS COGNOSCITIS
fte ic am
QUIA EGO SUM
infeden minu
INPATRE MEO
y gie onmec y ic
ET UOS INME ET EGO
in ivh
INUOBIS
red haped bebodo
QUI HABET MANDATA
mino y gehaldap hia tda
MEA ET SERUAT EA
he ir rede lyfap mec
ILLE EST QUI DILIGIT ME
rede vyt lyfap mec
QUI AUTEM DILIGIT ME

monastery of Wearmouth and Jarrow. This monastery, a centre in the area of Roman influence, was founded in 685 by Benedict Biscop, who visited Rome on seven occasions during his lifetime, returning with many objects, books and paintings. The scribe also approached the decoration of the manuscript in an innovative way. When laying out its structure he uses a new technique of lead point underdrawing and some kind of transparent writing desk (to see his designs which are drawn on the other side of the vellum). In a further example of change the text adopted for the Gospels was not the one used in other Irish-influenced manuscripts up to this date. Instead, it was the most up-to-date version or translation of the gospels, originally from an Italian copy, and perhaps also borrowed from Wearmouth. Other original features in the book include the classically influenced colour scheme which contrasts with the russets, autumnal reds, brown and green of earlier book's from the Lindisfarne scriptorium. The dominant colours of the Lindisfarne Gospels are pinks and purples, along with vibrant shades of green and strong blues.

A particularly fascinating feature is the blend of runic, Greek , Latin and invented letterforms in the principal headings of each gospel (forms also seen on grave markers made for the Lindisfarne community). Recent work by Michelle Brown at the British Library has uncovered up to sixty lead point under-drawings in the book, which indicate that many of these initials were originally intended simply to be enlarged forms of the main half-uncial text letters. A change of plan, involving a mix of forms, would therefore seem to be a deliberate artistic statement. In Michelle Brown's view this suggests that the scribe was making a visual statement concerning the unification of the various streams of Christian orthodoxy lived by the church in Northumbria at that time, which made it both distinctly local and universal. This is not a Celtic, Columban or Irish book as opposed to a Roman one, but in fact one that is consciously stating a unified position beyond these disputatious divisions.

A unifying vision

45

Out of something old…

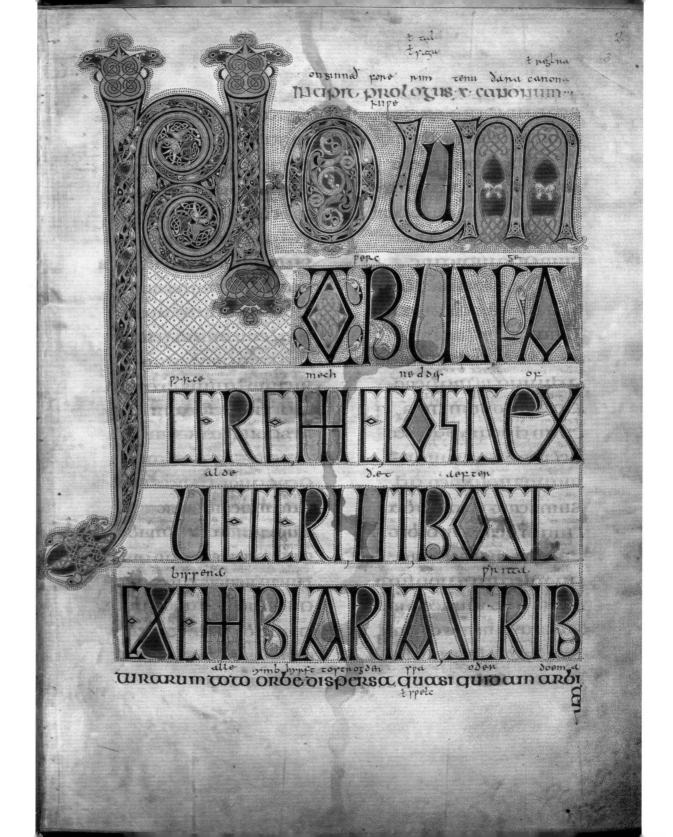

46

All these developments only underline just how remarkably Eadfrith, the scribe of ninety percent of the Gospel book, has blended the new with the old. He has not produced an awkward juxtaposition of competing influences, but a genuine transformation of his sources, Insular, Germanic and Roman, so that the overall effect is one of poise and balance rather than static solidity or crowded restlessness. He is deliberately taking on 'newness' across a breathtaking range of issues.

This approach to understanding Eadfrith's intentions is supported by one further observation. In another break with convention he chooses not to open his manuscript's decorative scheme with St. Matthew's Gospel. Instead, his first decorated page is a letter written by St. Jerome to Pope Damasus. This preface had appeared in Gospel books before (it was in the Book of Durrow) but here it has been elevated to the decorative magnificence of a gospel page itself. I felt a tingle down my spine when I read the opening words *'Novum opus facere me cogis ex veteri'* which mean, 'Out of something old, you compelled me to make something new'. Placed as they are at the very beginning of the book, marked out in this exceptional way, it is hard not to read these words in any other way than as a manifesto, a declaration of the community's vision and intent in the making of this manuscript.

What we see here, and there are many other technical factors I have not listed, is a remarkable openness to innovation and change that moves forward by combining disparate elements rather than sweeping them away. Eadfrith's achievement is to forge a new unity out of previously disparate elements and influences. This is also the role in which Bede casts Cuthbert in his *Ecclesiastical History*. He portrays him as someone who bridged two traditions, as he steered an Irish based community towards a new English understanding of church and community.

Let us make something new…

To describe the many innovations in the Lindisfarne Gospel Book as changes is to help us realize that they are likely to have had some community dimension to them. Whilst we know that most books from the Lindisfarne scriptorium are similar to the Lindisfarne Gospel Book in that they are largely the product of one individual, recent practical observation of the making of the great Bible commissioned for the monastery of St. John's in the USA convinces me that, however much the scribe may have seen his daily work as a personal consecration, this project must have implied some wider community involvement. Firstly it would have involved the monastery in a huge financial commitment. This was a costly book. One hundred and twenty-nine calf skins, rare pigments and gold were all used in its production. Only the community could have agreed to such expenditure or to the acceptance of such a gift from an outside donor (the possibility of strings being attached to gifts always make large gifts a community consideration). Only the community, too, could have assented to the expenditure of time which the scribe would need to have invested in the project, because it would clearly have implications for the division of work and responsibilities.

The nature of change itself also makes it highly unlikely that any one individual could have brought about such innovation on his own. People generally, and especially those in institutions (such as monasteries), resist change. It seems unlikely that Eadfrith the scribe would have imposed so many innovations without consultation when this book was designed to be a central artefact in Cuthbert's cult and used in the community's most important liturgical celebrations. This expectation of community involvement is strengthened by our knowledge of the way in which Eadfrith consulted the community during the production of another artefact crucial to the cult of Cuthbert: the prose *Life of Cuthbert* produced at Eadfrith's request. For two days (and after frequent consultations), it seems that Bede, its author, may have read his work to the whole assembled community, who commented upon it. From all this, it would seem that decisions

concerning the liturgical usefulness of a book such as the Lindisfarne Gospels are unlikely to have been made by the scribe in isolation. Informal consultation is likely also to have extended to aspects of the manuscript's decorative scheme, including the choice of passages that called for special treatment. On a practical level, too, alongside the scribe there would have been a team of workmen responsible for sourcing the animal skins for the vellum, making the vellum and then preparing it, perhaps even ruling up, collating and erasing. For the Lindisfarne scriptorium to have adopted so many changes within a single manuscript makes it almost certain that the involvement – and support – of the wider community was required. This being so, the impressive amount and quality of innovation present in the Lindisfarne Gospels suggest that the community as a whole, and not just the scribe, was also able to engage creatively with change.

So, the next question to ask is how the scribe and community achieved the inner alignment of attitude and spirit of which this book's art is a reflection. What patterns of behaviour or attitudes made this unusual degree of openness to change possible? How were they enabled to take on the promise of newness in such a remarkably creative and balanced way? The beginning of an answer to this lies, perhaps, in their spiritual inheritance from Cuthbert, who had reformed this community. We have already seen that he demonstrated gifts of reconciliation and healing and that he clearly had a deep understanding of the radical quality of mercy. Mercy, in the Christian understanding, breaks into the logic of cause and effect with a completely illogical gift that unlocks the inevitability of the system (this, incidentally, offers one way of understanding the deliberate 'mistakes' in certain decorative details of the Gospels' pages, in which the decorative system is never quite closed – look again at the birds' wings in the illustration on the previous page). Given the fact that *forgiveness* is perhaps the most important alignment of behaviour for the reception of change and the integration of the new, I think that we can see that the influence of Cuthbert's own spiritual practice may well have contributed directly to the parallel 'achievement of the spirit' that made the Lindisfarne Gospel Book artistically possible.

I would like to suggest that Cuthbert's influence on the way the community handled change must have begun to have been absorbed during that long period when he so moderately and skillfully helped the monks to come to terms with the decisions of the Synod of Whitby and to incorporate a more regular form of monastic life. Perhaps it was as he waited patiently until everyone was ready to move forward together that his community came to believe that, far from being a threat, change actually offered the promise of new life.

A completely illogical gift

The many artistic innovations visible throughout the Lindisfarne Gospel Book are evidence that, when the Lindisfarne community eventually decided to engage with change, they united in imitation of their leader, embracing it in a wonderfully moderate and skilful way. They were able to open themselves to the future without abruptly rejecting the past because this was already their practice among themselves as Christian souls and as a Christian community. They had already learned how to incorporate and honour the past, without ever allowing it to close their minds to what was fresh, vital and different, or to prevent them from engaging with 'the promise of newness'. This was simply a matter of daily experience.

And what of Eadfrith the scribe himself? He seems to have been a significant figure in the life of the community during the period of its increasing preoccupation with Cuthbert's memory. The figure of St. John on the coffin made for the translation of Cuthbert's remains in 698 has the same unique pose as his portrait in the gospel book. Perhaps Eadfrith the artist was involved in making the coffin also. And in later years, now as Abbot and Bishop of Lindisfarne (he was consecrated in the year of Cuthbert's translation) it was he who commissioned a life of Cuthbert from Bede.

All books focus some part of a community's life and activity. The evidence presented here suggests that Eadfrith was looking to bring out the 'Cuthbert element' of his community's life. Perhaps this was because it was threatened, as indeed it seems to have been during the brief unhappy period after Cuthbert's death when Wilfrid – the arch-Romanizer – took over in temporary charge of the monastery. There was a history here. Cuthbert's first responsibility had been as guest master at the newly established monastery at Ripon, founded by monks from Melrose at the invitation of a member of the Northumbrian royal house. The young Wilfrid, afire with youthful enthusiasm from a time spent in Rome, convinced the monastery's patron that it should be run in a more explicitly Roman manner. As a result, the monks from Melrose, Cuthbert included, were thrown out and Wilfrid was allowed to take over. Ripon became his ecclesiastical base. There he built an elaborate church and lived in considerable splendour. He was in fact everything that Cuthbert and Lindisfarne were not. Bede hints darkly that this year's interregnum was a time of very great difficulty for the Lindisfarne community. The irony was that Wilfrid, as a young man, had begun his religious life and education on Holy Island – perhaps there was a personal history here also.

And so after this period of difficulty the experience of Cuthbert's presence in the community began to be elaborated upon. He stood for something: humanity before rules, lack of pretension, the reconciling power of a compassionate God. His hard-won knowledge of human nature made him accessible, warm-hearted, humorous, forgiving, his presence was healing. He had a knack for empathy and an unmistaken insight, an infectious optimism. And just as anyone could approach him, so the evidence is that he, also, approached his God directly and vigorously. His brethren remembered him getting up in the night to take walks around the island, no doubt enjoying the solitude he later took as his entire way of life. They also remember him walking around 'Cuthbert's Island' singing. On a number of occasions they recalled him wading into the sea to pray, and on his death bed he raised his arms to greet the coming Christ. He had a great faith in the power of prayer. When he learned the community at Melrose had been praying for him all night because he had the plague, he immediately rose from his bed saying 'Then what am I lying here for? God will certainly have heard the prayers of so many good men.' Lindisfarne's tradition is about all this, it is a matter of values, an engagement with life and lessons learnt. It is the signs of this experience that make The Lindisfarne Gospels truly magnificent.

It was the community's duty to proclaim Cuthbert's sanctity; this was the way saints were made in the early Middle Ages. The Gospel Book is part of that process and witnesses to the extraordinary energy and devotion on which that work could draw. Then, as now, pilgrims came to the place where the holy man lived and was buried. We too come in search of a source of hope and love and healing in our lives – and perhaps to give thanks for all that enables us to engage with the unfolding promise of newness in our own lives, a promise we see so daringly explored and expressed in the making of this great manuscript book, a promise that remains available to this day.

Change is an ongoing process

Tide in
Tide out

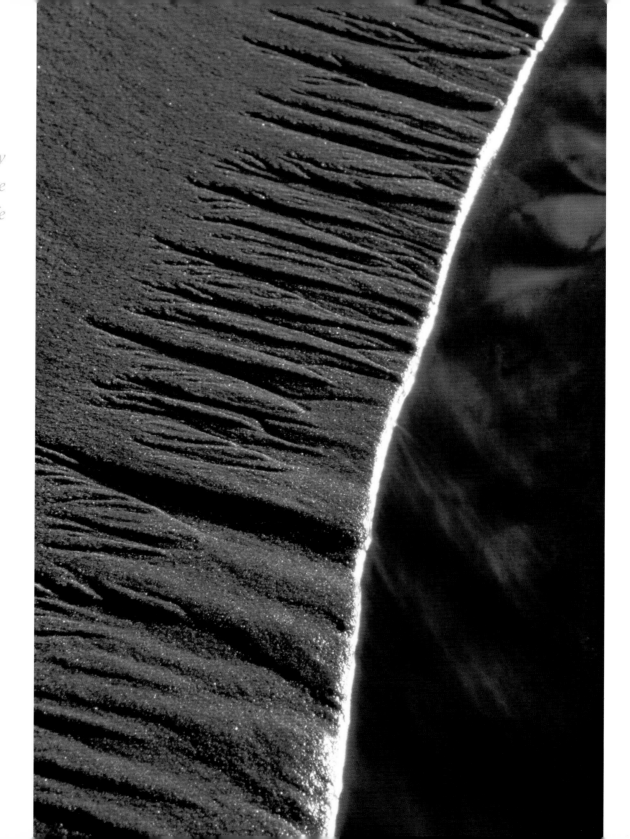

*Ready
to engage
with life*

Postscript

Change is an ongoing process and it is easy for a community apparently to embrace it, only for its members to realise later that they have simply substituted one way of being with another equally static, though different, way of life. Could this have been the case on Lindisfarne? There were rumours later in the eighth century that this community was growing slack, too wealthy and powerful. But a century after Cuthbert's death the Vikings struck. The first place they raided in the British Isles was Lindisfarne. The shock was felt across Europe. Alcuin, raised in the Cathedral school at York and now working as the teacher to the Court school of the Emperor Charlemagne, wrote, 'never before has such a terror appeared in Britain…nor was it thought possible that such an inroad from the sea could be made. Behold the Church of Cuthbert spattered with the blood of the priests of God…a place more venerable than all in Britain is given as a prey to pagan peoples.'

The community's response after several further raids over the following decades was an astonishing one. Eventually they resolved that the time had come for them to leave the island that had been their home for over two centuries. Taking their most precious possessions with them, including Cuthbert in his coffin and the famous Gospel Book, they took to the roads of Northumbria. The 'congregation of St. Cuthbert', as they came to be called, were led by their Bishop. They were a collection of monks, priests, laymen and families, and seven of the young men were specially appointed to be the bearers of St. Cuthbert. For well over a hundred years they moved across northern Britain, settling occasionally, but eventually on the move again until they found a final home. Through this uncertain time the community stuck together, appearing to accept change in such a way that it remained a community able to engage with life, even running to meet it – a fertile, self-renewing community that, in time, came to find a new home and to make a new beginning – in the place we now know as the Cathedral city of Durham.

Ewan Clayton writes:

This text was originally written for a study day on The Lindisfarne Gospels held at the British Library in 1999. It was revised and expanded during the autumn of 2002. My intention was to write about a manuscript from the point of view of the maker. As a calligrapher I wanted to stress that what is vital for our work is not only the techniques we use (most books about the Lindisfarne Gospels write about this), but why we do something and *what on a human level enables us to arrive at these choices and motivations.* This question approaches the source of creativity and it is on this level that the Lindisfarne Gospels speak to me. This project is one part of a wider work of finding a place for calligraphy in our contemporary society; demonstrating that it forms a contemplative practise in its own right and re-evoking the centering presence and eloquent reality of focal things from calligraphy's past by placing them once again in the public forum of celebration and the kinship of the focussed life. My thanks for their inspiration and help goes to Robert Cooper, Barbara Vellacott, Ian and Clare Clayton, Sue Hartridge, David Hole and to all those who have come on the retreats on Holy Island which Robert and I began in 1988. I am also indebted to those I count as my teachers on this path amongst whom I number Irene Wellington, Ann Camp, Julian Brown, Simon Harkin and the community of Worth Abbey.

Robert Cooper writes:

Just like the metaphor with which this book opens, the process of making it has been a journey. Such a journey encourages one to look back and to remember those who have influenced the direction it has taken. As amateur photographers, my father and grandfather must take first place alongside Warwick Metcalfe, my art teacher. He was the one who drew what talent I had out of me. Like Ewan, I also wish to thank Kate Tristram, Barbara Vellacott, those who have shared in the calligraphy retreats and the members of the Marygate community on Holy Island with whom we stay. All in their various ways have enlarged my vision and enriched my life. My gratitude also goes to my colleagues in the Arts and Recreation Chaplaincy, who have supported and encouraged my work. But it is Ewan himself who has been the deepest influence and I count his friendship and the invitation to share in the making of this book as among the greatest privileges of my life.

I am a calligrapher as well as a photographer. My work in both media involves pattern, texture and line – line in particular. The picture of the kelp on page 29, for example, is dominated by a single, calligraphic line. As a photographer, my chief influence has been Edward Weston, but it is Holy Island itself which remains my greatest inspiration. The landscapes in this book attempt to give some idea of the spaciousness of the place, its light and the powerful patterns created by sand and sea. The smaller details speak of something else - that, for me, the camera has become a way of contemplation. As I look through the lens sand, seaweed, driftwood, rock and the piles of discarded fishing tackle around the harbour and at the tide's edge are revealed in their unusual beauty. The "thisness" of these simple and apparently unimportant things transforms them into treasures of infinite value – and it is this that my photographs seek to celebrate.

Work of sight is done
 now do heart work
on the pictures within you

RILKE

LIST 0F ILLUSTRATIONS